THE CIVILIZATION OF THE AMERICAN INDIAN SERIES

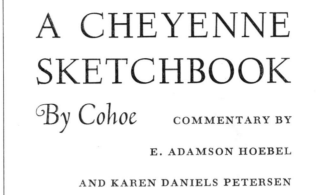

A CHEYENNE SKETCHBOOK

By Cohoe   COMMENTARY BY

E. ADAMSON HOEBEL

AND KAREN DANIELS PETERSEN

University of Oklahoma Press   :   Norman

A *Cheyenne Sketchbook* has been printed on paper intended
to have an effective life of three hundred years.

LIBRARY OF CONGRESS CATALOG CARD NUMBER: 64–21708

Copyright 1964 by the University of Oklahoma Press, Publishing Division of the
University. Composed and printed at Norman, Oklahoma, U.S.A., by the University of Oklahoma Press. First edition.

This book is dedicated to the Florida Boys

Acknowledgments

THE CO-OPERATIVE NATURE of the research required for this book is indicated by the length of the list of contributors. Space will permit only a partial listing of those who supplied, directly or indirectly, the data used in the text.

Generosity far beyond the call of duty characterized the assistance of the following: the Science Museum, St. Paul, Minnesota, and the University of Minnesota—for sponsorship of the research by contributing time and facilities; the American Philosophical Society, Penrose Fund—for a grant in support of the work, permitting the necessary travel; Jared Daniels Hill—for the gift of Cohoe's original sketchbook; Sidney A. Petersen—for assistance in field work in Oklahoma; the family of General Richard H. Pratt (Mrs. S. Clark Seelye, Edgar N. Hawkins, Richard Pratt, and Mrs. Richard Taylor)—for unstinted use of the General's papers; the Minnesota Historical Society (Lois M. Fawcett and others)—for access to manuscripts, pictures, and their notably complete library; Harry L. Deupree—for entrée into research in Oklahoma; the Hampton Institute staff—for ferreting out traces of the Florida Boys' student days; the Oklahoma Historical Society (Mrs. Rella Looney and others)—for records of the early agency; the University of Oklahoma and its Libraries (A. M. Gibson and others)—for information on obscure details; the Cheyenne-Arapaho Area Field office staff—for Indian Bureau records; the Smithsonian Institution, Bureau of American Ethnology (Mrs. Margaret C. Blaker and others)—for continued assistance from their manuscript files; and the National Archives staff—for old papers of the Indian Bureau.

Notable, also, in many ways was the help of the following: the American Museum of Natural History staff—for access to the Museum's Indian collections; Mrs. D. R. Bauman—for tracking down the Whipple sketchbooks; Mrs. Bruce Cohoe—for data on William Cohoe; Mrs. Charles Curtis—for assistance in field work; Claude E. Hensley—for the use of his manuscript collection; Sam Maffett—for the use of family papers; the Missouri Historical Society staff—for leads on Fort Marion art; Mrs. Rodolphe Petter—for data from her husband's Cheyenne dictionary; Roy H. Robinson—for access to his sketchbooks; the St. Augustine Historical Society (Doris C. Wiles)—for photographs and data on Fort Marion prisoners; and the Southwest Museum (Mrs. Ella Robinson)—for the use of manuscript collections.

Deserving of more than the simple enumeration that space allows are Richard T. Anderson, Joseph Balmer, Jay Black, the Chicago Natural History Museum (George I. Quimby), Angie Debo, Dorothy Dunn, Mrs. Standing Twenty Good Bear, Mrs.

Mary Inkanish, John C. Ewers, Crooked Nose Flying Bird, the James J. Hill Reference Library staff, James H. Howard, René d'Harnoncourt, George E. Hyde, Elden Johnson, Gertrude Kurath, the Library of Congress staff, Alice Marriott, the Massachusetts Historical Society (Stephen T. Riley), the Museum of New Mexico (Wayne L. Mauzy), the Museum of the American Indian (Heye Foundation) (Frederick J. Dockstader and others), the National Museum of Canada (L. S. Russell), The New York Public Library staff, Mrs. Mary Rambull, Howard D. Rodee, the St. Louis *Post-Dispatch* (Roy T. King), the St. Paul Public Library staff, the United States National Museum of Natural History (T. Dale Stewart and others), Mrs. Samuel Tyler, Mrs. Richanda Stone Calf, the U.S. Department of the Interior (Office of Indian Affairs) (John F. Carmody), the U.S. Department of the Interior (National Park Service, Castillo de San Marcos National Monument) (Luis R. Arana); the U.S. Department of the Interior (Region 1) (John W. Griffin), the University of Minnesota Library, Anthony Walsh, Mrs. A. W. J. Watt, and the Yale University Library (Western Americana Division) (Archibald Hanna).

The editors express their heartfelt thanks to all these who gave indispensable help in piecing together, bit by bit, the scattered fragments of the story of Cohoe and his sketches.

E. ADAMSON HOEBEL

KAREN DANIELS PETERSEN

September 26, 1964

Contents

Acknowledgments   ix

Introduction   3

PART ONE: LIFE ON THE PLAINS—HUNTING

     I. *Pronghorns and Turkeys*   25

     II. *The Elk Hunt*   29

     III. *Buffalo*   35

     IV. *Flaying the Buffalo*   39

PART TWO: LIFE ON THE PLAINS—CEREMONIES

     V. *The Sun Dance*   43

     VI. *Wolf Soldiers*   49

     VII. *The Honoring*   55

     VIII. *The Feast*   61

     IX. *The Osage Dancers*   67

PART THREE: LIFE AT FORT MARION—PRISONERS OF WAR

     X. *Anastasia Island*   73

     XI. *Water Buffalo*   79

     XII. *War Dance at Fort Marion*   85

Catalogue of the Art of the Indians Imprisoned
     at Fort Marion, Florida, 1875–78   91

Index   94

Illustrations

BETWEEN PAGES 16 AND 17

Nohnicas or Cohoe / Fort Marion / Cheyenne Prisoners on Arrival / Cohoe and His Fellow Cheyennes / Hampton Institute / Three Cheyenne Delegates / Bishop Henry Benjamin Whipple / Cheyenne Painted Buffalo Robe

Pronghorns and Turkeys	23	The Honoring	53
The Elk Hunt	27	The Feast	59
Buffalo	33	The Osage Dancers	65
Flaying the Buffalo	37	Anastasia Island	71
The Sun Dance	41	Water Buffalo	77
Wolf Soldiers	47	War Dance at Fort Marion	83

XV

Introduction

W HEN HE GOT LONESOME, he drew pictures about relatives
and the things he would remember."[1] The sketches that consti-
tute the heart of this book were the eloquent outlet for a slender
Cheyenne, who in his early manhood had been forcibly removed
from his beloved Plains and their colorful life of movement and
action to the confines of a hundred-year-old Spanish fort in that
most ancient of American cities, St. Augustine, Florida. He was
a warrior, one of the last of the fighters to succumb to the power
of American military might and the settlement of the Southern
Plains.

In 1874 many of the Southern Cheyennes placed their trust
in a Comanche messiah who claimed to have been given the
power to endow himself and any who would follow him with
immunity to bullets. He promised that should they hearken to
his word, the intruding whites would be wiped from the face of

---

[1] Mrs. Standing Twenty Good Bear, oral communication to Karen Daniels
Petersen, May 18, 1959.

3

the Plains. They would begin with the hated buffalo hunters—the annihilators of the Indians' food supply—working out of the frontier post at Adobe Walls, Texas. Comanches, Kiowas, and Cheyennes, embittered and desperate, listened with a mounting fervor of hope, and the war flame burned anew. Disaster at Adobe Walls on the morning of June 27, 1874, dashed their hopes, and nothing was left but the prospect of the frustrating lassitude of reservation life.

A few unyielding fighters continued, nonetheless, to vent their feelings in fitful marauding depredations and killings that terrorized the Southern frontier throughout the rest of the year. Among them was a young Southern Cheyenne, who followed the leadership of Medicine Water. His name was Mohe, meaning "Elk," or Mapera-mohe, "Water Elk" or "Moose." He had been born in what is now Colorado, about 1854, son of Sleeping Bear and Plain Looking.[2]

Relentlessly harried by campaigning troopers, suffering from the inclemency of an extremely bitter winter, with no time to get food, their ponies weakened, and their lodges destroyed, the resistance fighters ultimately had no choice but to capitulate. At the close of the year, Mohe and his friend, Bear's Heart, came into the agency to surrender themselves. Official reports record their surrender as having occurred variously on December 12,

[2] Cheyenne-Arapaho Area Field Office, Concho, Oklahoma (hereinafter cited as Concho), Allotment file No. 2728, Mrs. Amos Chapman. Sleeping Bear was killed in the massacre of Black Kettle's camp of friendly Cheyennes by Colonel J. M. Chivington's Colorado militia at Sand Creek, 1864.

19, or 20, 1874. They had then been with the camp of Grey Beard, a chief of the Sutai Band of Cheyennes.

At the Darlington agency Mohe was identified by Big Moccasin as a member of the war party that had fallen upon a family by the name of German, killing the parents and three children and abducting four girls. He was also alleged to have been among those who had assaulted and killed the Short party of six surveyors. On this information, he was reported as being held under close guard on January 3.[3] His days as a free Indian were over.

The United States was determined to make an indelible example of the hostile chiefs and their accomplices. No mass executions, such as had followed the Sioux outbreak in Minnesota a decade before, were contemplated, but it was decided to subject the offenders to transportation and incarceration in an Eastern prison. At first there was to be a trial before the military commission, but in the end even this simple amenity of justice was set aside. In the case of the Cheyennes, the army merely selected for imprisonment four principal chiefs and leaders along with eight warriors who had been named as alleged participants in the German and Short killings, plus three who were held to have been implicated in the Brown killings. One of the eight

[3] Agent J. D. Miles to Commissioner Smith, letters dated December 12, 1874, Central Superintendency Field Papers, Cheyenne and Arapaho, 1874; December 22, 1874, Letters Received, Upper Arkansas Agency, 1874; January 3, 1875, Letters Received, Cheyenne and Arapaho Agency, 1875, in U.S. National Archives, Record Group 75, Bureau of Indian Affairs.

was a woman. Eighteen others were simply cut off from the end of the line of "arraigned" Cheyennes to round out the complement of those to be imprisoned at thirty-three.

Mohe was entered in the official reports of January as "Limpy"; when the prisoner lists of April 29 and May 17, 1875, were compiled, he appeared as "Cohoe."[4] This is not a Cheyenne personal name, but it was a widespread sobriquet deriving from the Spanish *"cojo,"* meaning "lame." Cohoe was in no sense a cripple, but, as was usual among the Cheyennes, he had either taken a new name as an adult or received a nickname from his intimates. The U.S. National Museum list accompanying the casts of the facial masks of the prisoners identifies him as "Broken Leg, Cohoe." Later, at Hampton Institute he acquired a dignified Cheyenne equivalent of Cohoe—"Nohnicas," or "Cripple." And finally, when at last he returned to Indian Territory, he had an English surname, William, signing himself "William Cohoe," "Cohoe," or by thumbprint in letters and agency documents, 1881–1924.

After assembling at Fort Sill in Indian Territory, seventy-two prisoners, Cheyenne, Arapaho, Kiowa, Comanche, and Caddo, started the long journey to Fort Marion in Florida late in April, 1875. The harshness of their fate was ameliorated by a

---

[4] Miles to Smith, letter dated April 29, 1875, National Archives, Record Group 75, Bureau of Indian Affairs; Assistant Adjutant General Williams, synopsis showing names of Indian prisoners and charges against them, Fort Leavenworth, Kansas, May, 1875, General Richard H. Pratt Papers (hereinafter cited as Pratt Papers), Yale University, New Haven, Conn., Beinecke Rare Book and Manuscript Library, Western Americana Collection.

small show of official compassion, which had allowed the request of Lieutenant Richard H. Pratt that he be assigned the duty of their safeguard. Pratt, who had served with distinction in the Indian campaigns as commander of Indian and white scouts with the Fort Sill column, now hoped to be the instrument of the prisoners' rehabilitation as civilized men adapted to life in the white man's world. He was a true humanitarian who devoted his indefatigable energies thenceforth to the promotion of Indian well-being and advancement, earning a well-deserved immortality as "the Red Man's Moses."

At the prison in St. Augustine, "Captain" Pratt (as he was universally called) encouraged his charges to practice such skills as could be fostered. One outlet for self-expression that was fully utilized was in drawing and painting. Almost all Plains Indian males had some experience in depicting their exploits in hide painting in a traditional manner. Although the prisoners received no instruction in sketching at Fort Marion, within a month after their arrival some of them were drawing to pass the time away and earn pocket money.

The sketchbook from which the scenes in this volume were selected was sent to Bishop Henry Benjamin Whipple of Minnesota by Captain Pratt as a memento of the Bishop's visit to Fort Marion in 1876. But it was more than a memento; it was an expression of gratitude and love offered by the Captain and his Indian charges. For the lives of the Indian captives and the hopes of Captain Pratt for the renewal of their lives within the framework of civilization were deeply touched by the Bishop.

Elected the first Protestant Episcopal bishop of the frontier diocese of Minnesota in 1859, Henry Whipple had at once seen for himself, on a journey to an Indian mission, the calamitous effect of the government's policies. Thenceforth he bombarded Washington officials—even the President—with eloquent letters voicing his burning sympathy for the victims of Manifest Destiny.

In 1862, even as his warnings had foreshadowed, the Sioux of Minnesota plunged into one of the most disastrous Indian uprisings in our country's history. Bishop Whipple gave President Lincoln a man-to-man account of the causes of the outbreak and its results for the Sioux. Of the three hundred Indians who had been condemned to death the President pardoned all but thirty-nine.

For the next few years "Straight Tongue," as the Indians called the Bishop, pressed the battle for his "red children" with countless speeches and letters in the East and abroad. Indian sympathizers besieged him for aid, advice, and addresses. Funds poured in for the schools and Indian missions which he had established.

Old residents of St. Augustine who recalled a winter he spent among them at the beginning of his ministry had followed his progress with pride and had learned from his example. So it was that when Cohoe and the other captives arrived at the fort, the *Florida Press* editorially welcomed them with a stirring résumé of injustices suffered by Indians. Mentioning "the few clergy who have labored among them," the writer added, "and

8

foremost among the latter we must not forget that eminent, whole-souled champion of the Indian, Bishop Whipple, of Minnesota, whilom Rector of our own little church, whose evidence is conviction itself."[5]

Early in the spring of 1876, the Bishop made the long journey from Faribault, Minnesota, to St. Augustine to recoup his health, and remained to lend support to Captain Pratt's rehabilitation efforts. He preached nine times to the prisoners, his words being translated in sign language as he spoke. So great was his impress that Pratt wrote subsequently: "They seldom make a drawing book without putting you in. The Bishop talking to them, the classes and teachers: and their line as soldiers are three staple pictures."[6]

Toward the end of the Bishop's stay, the residents of St. Augustine put on a spectacular entertainment for the winter resorters, "The Grand Gala Day!!" A regatta in the bay and sporting contests on land culminated in an Indian war dance at the fort (Plate Twelve).

While still at St. Augustine, Bishop Whipple was the recipient of one or more picture books made by the captives. These he apparently gave away with his characteristic openhandedness, so he wrote to Captain Pratt asking for more.[7]

[5] "The Indian Question," St. Augustine *Florida Press* (June 5, 1875).

[6] Letter dated San Marco, July 26, 1876, Bishop Henry B. Whipple Papers (hereinafter cited as Whipple Papers), Minnesota Historical Society, St. Paul, Minn.

[7] Letter dated On River, March 15, 1876, Pratt Papers; H. B. Whipple to R. H. Pratt, letter dated Faribault, Minn., August 22, 1876, Pratt Papers; H. B. Whipple to R. H. Pratt, letter dated On Cars, November 13, [1876], Pratt Papers.

Pratt complied with the Bishop's first request for a book.[8] Later he reported: "Several good books are in progress. Will send one when done."[9] On July 31, Pratt recorded in the front of one sketchbook the place and date of its completion, as was the wont of this army-trained man, inscribing it to "Bishop Whipple—With compliments and regards of R. H. Pratt U.S.A."

While preparing to set out for two months of treating with the Sioux, the Bishop replied to Captain Pratt's offer: "I shall be glad to get one of their drawing books for myself and one for a friend."[10]

In December, Pratt wrote again: "I sent you five of the best books I could find. The price is $2.00 each."[11] Among these was the July 31 book.

The other four were dated September, 1876. Cohoe's sketch-book is one of this latter group.[12] After eighty years it came into the possession of Karen Daniels Petersen, a gift of her cousin Jared Daniels Hill, of Los Angeles, California. He had found the treasure among the family relics bequeathed to him by his

[8] Letter dated Fort Marion, March 20, 1876, Whipple Papers.

[9] Letter dated San Marco, July 26, 1876, Whipple Papers.

[10] Letter dated Faribault, Minn., August 22, 1876, Pratt Papers.

[11] Letter dated St. Augustine, Fla., December 21, [1876], Whipple Papers.

[12] The other four are in the private collection of Roy H. Robinson, Chicago, Illinois. At the back of the July 31 book, in the Bishop's hand, is the inscription, "To my beloved Evangeline with her husband's love H. B. Whipple." Subsequent to his first wife's death in 1890, he had married Evangeline in 1896. When his library was to be disposed of in 1933, thirty-two years after his death, Mrs. D. R. Bauman of Minneapolis discovered these four behind a row of books in the Bishop's study. Mrs. D. R. Bauman, oral communication to Karen Daniels Petersen, March, 1959.

widowed mother Hortense, who had brought them to California from Faribault, Minnesota, in 1923. Nothing more was known about its history, except for a bold-handed inscription in the book itself: "Drawn by Cohoe (Cheyenne) Ft Marion Fla. Sept. 1876."

Below the inscription a bookplate admonished, "Kindly return when perused"; it further identified the volume as "number one" in the library of H. B. Hill, whose name was inscribed at the top of the page. The bookplate was that of Henry Benjamin Hill, namesake of Bishop Whipple and onetime resident of Faribault, Minnesota (the Bishop's see), and son of the Bishop's sister Susan.

Bishop Whipple's second request of Captain Pratt had been for "one of their drawing books for myself and one for a friend." Of one man the Bishop said at various times: "My very dear friend, Dr. J. W. Daniels, who loved the Indians and knew their language";[13] "I knew of no one who had a more intelligent acquaintance with the problem of Indian civilization";[14] and, "one of the purest and best men I ever knew."[15]

[13] H. B. Whipple, "Address," *Proceedings of the Eleventh Annual Meeting of the Lake Mohonk Conference of the Friends of the Indian, 1893* (N.p., 1893), 36.

[14] H. B. Whipple, letter dated Faribault, November 24, [1886], in "Kind Words for Gen, [*sic*] Sibley," St. Paul and Minneapolis *Daily Pioneer Press* (November 26, 1886), 1.

[15] H. B. Whipple to Commissioner N. G. Taylor, extracts from letter dated Faribault, December 10, 1868, enclosed in letter of the Commissioner of Indian Affairs transmitted in Letter of the Secretary of the Interior, U.S. Congress, *Sen. Exec. Doc. No. 28*, 40 Cong., 3 sess., 1868–69 (Serial No. 1360), 3.

When the new Bishop visited the Lower Sioux Agency in 1860 preliminary to establishing the school for the Sioux advocated by their government physician, Dr. Asa Wilder Daniels, the latter's brother was physician to the Upper Sioux, only thirty miles away. In 1865, Dr. Jared Waldo Daniels located in Faribault for two years and became the Bishop's neighbor, his family physician, and a member of his congregation. Three years later when Congress, without the Bishop's knowledge, appropriated a large sum of money to be administered by him for the destitute Sisseton and Wahpeton Sioux, the overburdened cleric prevailed on Dr. Daniels to give up his practice in the city of St. Peter and act as his agent. In the early 1870's, on Bishop Whipple's recommendation, the doctor was appointed to fill in for the agent at the turbulent Red Cloud Agency. At the very time of the Bishop's letter to Pratt requesting sketchbooks, Bishop Whipple was at Faribault making the preparations necessary for a hazardous sixty-six days' journey in the company of Dr. Daniels. Together they served on the Sioux Commission to treat with the bands of the upper Missouri for their sacred Black Hills. Here was a friend desirous and deserving of the best of the Bishop's sketchbooks.[16]

16 *Ibid.*; George C. Tanner, *Fifty Years of Church Work in the Diocese of Minnesota* (St. Paul, Minn., 1909), 210; H. B. Whipple, *Lights and Shadows of a Long Episcopate* (New York, 1899), 60–61; "Personal," Faribault, Minn., *Central Republican* (November 27, 1867); [H. B. Whipple], Bishop's Letter, from Maitland, Fla., February 11, 1889, in *Minnesota Missionary and Church Record*, Vol. XIII, No. 3 (March, 1889), 36; Abstract of Letters Sent, Indian Commissioner, August 18, 1876 (Rec. 130–534) and August 26, 1876 (Rec. 130–555), National Archives, Bureau of Indian Affairs.

In 1895 the doctor's daughter Hortense was joined in marriage to the Bishop's nephew Henry. The book that had belonged to both his uncle and his father-in-law became "number one" in Henry Benjamin Hill's library.

In April, 1878, after three years of captivity, the "Florida Boys" were released from Fort Marion. Cohoe was one of seventeen who were then admitted to Hampton Institute in Virginia as the first Indian students at the Negro agricultural and industrial school.[17] There, in March, 1879, he and twelve other former prisoners were baptized and accepted into the brotherhood of Christianity. Toward the end of his year at Hampton he was reported thus, in an account of the school:

"In the girls' industrial department, a colored graduate is head tailor. He is cutting and pressing the neat gray uniforms of the students. Ko-hoe, a Cheyenne Indian, has learned with the greatest patience and zeal to run a sewing machine. Forty or fifty girls have made over a thousand articles, and mended innumerable others, and earned by wages, at the rate of from 25 to 40 cents per day, about $360."[18]

Cohoe, the marauding fighter of 1874, had become an apprentice tailor among fifty Negro girls in 1879. Later that summer, while a dozen of the Indians were working on farms in New England, he again appeared in the news as an energetic money-

[17] *Catalogue of the Hampton Normal and Agricultural Institute, Hampton, Virginia, for the Academical Year 1877–8* (Hampton, Va., 1878), 14.

[18] "Hampton Negro and Indian School"—date line, Hampton, Va., May 22, 1879—Springfield *Republican* (May 30, 1879).

maker. In the *Southern Workman* we read: "The [Lee, Massachusetts, Farmers'] club invited the Indians as guests, and all came but two, Cohoe and Soaring Eagle. Cohoe preferred to attend a pic-nic, at which a prize of $2.00 was offered for the best runner. Cohoe won the prize."[19]

Meanwhile Captain Pratt's vision and persistent energy brought about the dedication of the Carlisle, Pennsylvania, army barracks to the use of a boarding school for Indians. In October, 1879, the Florida Boys became the first enrollees, and Cohoe was among them. He was anxious to begin his life at home anew, however; for he was now twenty-six years old. Consequently, with two Kiowas and an Arapaho, accompanied by A. J. Standing, a Carlisle teacher who was to recruit students in the West, Cohoe left Carlisle for the Cheyenne and Arapaho Agency on March 2, 1880. The little party traveled three days by rail, and then four days by wagon after leaving the railroad.

After five years and three months as a prisoner and student, Cohoe was home again—a reformed Cheyenne.

The next year Agent J. D. Miles wrote to Captain Pratt of his erstwhile charges, reporting: "Cohoe is hard at work, exemplifying his faith in civilization . . . and working as white men do."[20] And in the same year Cohoe spoke for himself in a letter to a former teacher at Hampton Institute, saying: "I do not want

[19] "Indians in Berkshire County, Massachusetts," *Southern Workman*, Vol. VIII, No. 8 (August, 1879), 85.

[20] Letter dated Cheyenne and Arapaho Agency, Indian Territory, September 28, 1881, in *Annual Report of the Commissioner of Indian Affairs . . . 1881* (Washington, D. C., 1881), 193.

the Indian way any more. And the Cheyenne we are going to try to get the white man's road and to work hard in the farm all right way now."[21]

The records speak eloquently and poignantly of Cohoe's struggle to find his way along the white man's road. Three weeks after his return he was given work at the agency, first as a laborer, then as a mill hand, and later as a teamster, transporting supplies from the railroad to the agency. On October 7, 1881, he was nominated as a brick molder. He was appointed baker for the agency schools on December 1, 1881, "and with few exceptions," wrote Agent Miles three months later, "is making very good bread."[22] By July of 1882, however, Mason Pratt, who was visiting in Indian Territory, wrote his father that Cohoe had failed as a baker and had been removed from his post.[23]

According to Cohoe's own account, he also farmed and butchered for the agency and put in fences. After his discharge as baker, he quit employment at the agency and worked for six years or so as clerk in a local trading post.[24] After that he had a

[21] Letter to Miss L[udlow] dated Darlington, April 14, 1881, in *Hampton Normal and Agricultural Institute, Report of the Principal for 1881, and General Information* (Hampton, Va., 1882), 33.

[22] Letter to Commissioner H. Price, dated Cheyenne and Arapaho Agency, February 2, 1882, Cheyenne-Arapaho Agency Letter Book, September 2, 1881–February 2, 1882, p. 477, Indian Archives, Oklahoma Historical Society, Oklahoma City.

[23] Letter dated Cheyenne and Arapaho Agency, July 8, 1882, Pratt Papers.

[24] William Cohoe, reply to questionnaire, Record of Graduates and Returned Students, dated Bickford, Okla., December 15, 1910, Student Attendance Record No. 302, Carlisle Indian School, National Archives, Record Group 75, Bureau of Indian Affairs.

turn in the U.S. Army as a private in the scouts at Fort Supply from August 3, 1887, to August 2, 1888.[25] Thereafter he made his way, as many another Plains Indian has tried, as a small farmer.

When Cohoe had been taken away as a prisoner, he had left a young wife behind in the Cheyenne camps. Her name was Small Woman. She was waiting for him upon his return, and was still his faithful helpmate at his death forty-four years later. Cohoe was sustained through all his trials by what must have been one of the finest exemplars of Cheyenne womanhood. And it is clear that Cohoe himself was a solid husband, for, sometime after his return to the homeland, he was given Small Woman's younger sister, Pelican (or Surprise) Woman, also known as Vister, as a second wife in the old Cheyenne manner. He had a son, named Walking Coyote (Charles Cohoe), by Small Woman in 1882, two years after his return. Some three years later he had a second son, Black Bird (Bruce Cohoe), by Pelican Woman.[26] Two or three years later Pelican Woman deserted Cohoe for Stands in Timber, taking Black Bird with her. The redoubtable Small Woman would not have it, however; mounting her horse, she journeyed to Stands in Timber's camp. Taking Black Bird upon her horse "to go for a ride," she carried him back to Cohoe's home to raise his son and her nephew as her own.[27] Because she and Cohoe had no daughter, Small Woman also helped raise the

[25] Register of Enlistments for Indian Scouts, 1887–1914, National Archives, War Department, Record Group 94, Adjutant General's Office.

[26] Allotment file No. 1936, Cohoe, Concho.

[27] Mrs. Bruce Cohoe, oral communication to Karen Daniels Petersen, May 19, 1959.

NOHNICAS OR COHOE

CALLED LAME MAN

Bureau of American Ethnology, 1899

CASTILLO DE SAN MARCOS (FORT MARION)
ST. AUGUSTINE, FLORIDA, *c*. 1886

National Park Service

CHEYENNE PRISONERS, ON ARRIVAL AT FORT MARION, 1875

Yale University

COHOE (SECOND FROM RIGHT) WITH HIS FELLOW CHEYENNES
SOON AFTER ARRIVAL AT FORT MARION

Yale University

HAMPTON INSTITUTE, HAMPTON, VIRGINIA, 1878

Hampton Institute

THREE CHEYENNE DELEGATES DURING 1899 CHEYENNE-ARAPAHO
VISIT TO COMMISSIONER OF INDIAN AFFAIRS, WASHINGTON.
LEFT TO RIGHT: HENRY ROMAN NOSE (NOT TO BE CONFUSED
WITH ROMAN NOSE, D. 1868, BEECHER'S ISLAND);
YELLOW BEAR; AND COHOE

Bureau of American Ethnology, 1899

BISHOP HENRY BENJAMIN WHIPPLE
FREQUENT VISITOR TO THE
CHEYENNE PRISONERS, 1876.
RECEIVED COHOE'S SKETCHBOOK
FROM CAPTAIN PRATT.

Minnesota Historical Society

CHEYENNE PAINTED BUFFALO ROBE (1875?) SHOWING STATE OF
CHEYENNE ART IMMEDIATELY PRECEDING COHOE'S SKETCHBOOK

Denver Art Museum

daughter of another sister, who was married to a former prison-mate of Cohoe's, Little Chief, Bishop Whipple's staunchest pro-tégé.[28] Small Woman was not alone a faithful Cheyenne wife and loving mother; she also had a reputation as a fine bead and quill worker.[29]

Cohoe made no more paintings after he returned from his imprisonment in the East, except for doing bits "on *small* buffalo hides for children, which were ornamented by groups of men working together."[30] His need for nostalgic expression through the medium of art was gone. "He hardly talked about Florida," say those who remember him today.[31]

Cohoe struggled at his farming after 1891 upon his own land, which he received in allotment. He raised corn and put up hay every summer. At fifty-six he was still struggling along the white man's road. In his own words, he reported in 1910:

"I have two room House and have find [fine] fruit every year. Peaches apples cherries Grapes. Now at present I lived at my own land farmer every year I have all kinds of different fruits sell, and put a way for winter used.

"I have 4 head of Horse two room house and a stable. . . .

"For many years I am farming every year at this present time working out to make a living and support my wife. and wood to hauled in town. . . .

"But now I have no Imlp [implements] to work with now.

[28] Mrs. Richanda Little Chief Stone Calf, oral communication to Karen Daniels Petersen, May 22, 1959.

[29] Mrs. Cohoe, *loc. cit.*   [30] Mrs. Stone Calf, *loc. cit.*   [31] *Ibid.*

I go around borrowed them among different Indians just [such] as plow cultivator lister [a special plow] Gold devil [go-devil—a sled for logs]. . . . I have nothing to go a head and work with I work hard try to make a living, at the same time I am getting poor. . . . It looks I can not get started my wife and I both work out at all times. . . . I wante you to help me some way in regard about Imlp tools to work with every summer."[32]

In 1899 he was briefly in Washington as a member of a delegation of Cheyennes and Arapahos summoned to discuss the appointment of a defense attorney to handle threatened damage suits arising from earlier raids.

Cohoe's life of ill-rewarded effort held some relief in the color that survived in the readapted remnants of the life that once was. He found solace and vision in membership in the Peyote Cult, the Native American Church that developed among the Plains tribes in the days after defeat. He put Christianity behind him. And in his last years he was head chief of the Onihanotria, or War Dancers Society, the men's fraternity that had sprung from the dance that had gripped his imagination when imprisoned within the old stone walls of Fort Marion so far away and long ago.

In 1914, an old man of sixty, he gave up farming and leased all, or part, of his lands.[33] Ten years later friends and relatives gathered to him. Sitting up in bed, he dictated his will to the Agency Farmer, leaving eighty acres each to his only surviving

[32] William Cohoe, reply to questionnaire, *loc. cit.*
[33] Allotment file No. 1936, Cohoe, Concho.

child, Bruce Cohoe, and to his faithful wife, Small Woman.[34] Before the setting of the next sun, death came to Cohoe, on March 18, 1924, at his allotment in Blaine County, near Bickford, Oklahoma, after seven decades as untamed Cheyenne, prisoner of war, artist, schoolboy, laborer, soldier, and farmer.

His epitaph is spoken in the words of those who live today, the Southern Cheyennes, who say of him truly: "He was a good, kind man"[35]—"Well thought of among the people"[36] (*The people*—Tsistsistas, the Cheyennes' own name for themselves.) His sensitive reaching out for life speaks to us through the images which he has left behind in this, his sketchbook.

Cohoe's is not the only sketchbook that has survived from the days of his captivity. Others are listed at the end of this volume. But of all these which we have seen, the work of Cohoe excels in quality and in details of costume and regalia. Many worked with too small a page or too large a scene, or they did not use the effective device of showing a few to represent the many. Some were simply less skillful, some were careless, some were obviously interested in mass production for tourist consumption. True, a few told a more consecutive story, several absorbed more of the white man's art, and a number were many times more prolific, but none showed more love of the pageantry of the

[34] *Ibid.*

[35] Mrs. Mary Rambull, oral communication to Karen Daniels Petersen, May 18, 1959.

[36] Jay Black, keeper of the Sacred Arrows of the Cheyennes, oral communication to Karen Daniels Petersen, May 23, 1959.

Plains. Cohoe's sketches are suffused with the beautiful Cheyenne sentiment for remembering expressed in the eloquent
imagery of the Cheyenne metaphor, "I am sending my heart
back over the years." As we contemplate his pictures let us not
forget what moved him to portray the scenes of his mind's eye
upon the pages of the sketchbook—"When he got lonesome, he
drew pictures about relatives and the things he would remember."

What are the scenes of remembrance? We have grouped
them about three motifs. Two of them portray the old days:
hunting—the exciting and satisfying base of material subsistence;
and ritual participation—the ceremonial and spiritual base of
religious and social existence. The third centers on the new life
of captivity in which Cohoe's artistic representations reflect the
ghostly shadows of the cherished former life in pale transmuted
form—camping and shark-fishing in army garb without insignia
of company or regiment. The captives were in the custody of the
army but not a part of it. In place of the Sun Dance, and its
attendant military society dances and honorings, we see the
War Dance, a vicarious substitute for the manly activity now
denied the prisoners, a substitute which they were permitted to
perform within the confines of the prison walls for the titillation
of white spectators. A consistent theme runs through the scenes
of this little volume: a life that was once, glorified in riotous
color and selective elaboration of costumery, a nostalgic recon-
struction of the Golden Age of the Cheyennes; and the life that
was now to be endured. The somber blues and greens of "Anas-

tasia Island" and "Water Buffalo" (Plates Ten and Eleven) contrast darkly to the brilliant gaiety of all the previous scenes. The Cheyennes of Fort Marion were living, but the color had gone from their lives. A small spark of it is rekindled in "War Dance at Fort Marion" (Plate Twelve), but compare it with "The Osage Dancers" (Plate Nine), and our meaning will be clear.

Cohoe also pictured the symbols of the supremacy of the people who had conquered him, which, of course, impressed him by their very novelty: a steam locomotive, a sailing ship, and a side-wheeler steam vessel. We have not included these sketches in this volume, for they hold little intrinsic value.

PLATE ONE: PRONGHORNS AND TURKEYS

1.   *Pronghorns and Turkeys*

As a captive artist, imprisoned for his war record, Cohoe left no scenes of war or raid in his sketchbook. Yet he could not wholly repress his fervor for the Cheyenne warrior on horseback. Thus, in this picture a noble idealization of a successful attack on the open Plains is grandly portrayed. Most of the riders are armed and garbed for fighting rather than hunting. The leader rides a horse fully decorated in the "hail" war paint, and he carries a ceremonial medicine lance, which is hardly to be thought of as a hunting weapon. He is merely using it to touch, or count coup upon, the fleeing birds and beasts, which are being treated more as enemies in a sham attack than as game. The whole import of this scene is that of a mock war party.

The composition bears a strong resemblance to old-time hide paintings. In the conventions of the art a man was identifiable from his finery as he was in life. These are Cohoe's friends and confreres. It is likely that the Cheyenne prisoners, upon looking at this picture, could call each rider by name.

25

Cloven hoofs, banded breast, and forked horns clearly identify the pronghorn. The incongruously drawn turkeys reflect the
fact that turkeys were not a part of the old-time hide-painting
tradition; hence, Cohoe had no stylized pattern to follow such as
gave him the graceful delineation of running horses. He had to
invent his own depiction without much skill in free representation. But why put the turkeys in at all? We can imagine a true
antelope hunt in Cohoe's lost days on the Plains when a loping
herd of pronghorns and pursuing hunters overran a hidden flock
that just could not get out of the way. Phantasy war party and
scurrying turkeys became one.

PLATE TWO: THE ELK HUNT

11.   *The Elk Hunt*

In this leaping scene of two bedecked Cheyenne hunters riding down a fleeing herd of elk, Cohoe has combined the old and the new. The rider at the upper right sits astride his horse in the conventional manner of the old-style hide paintings. His arched-necked steed stretches full length in the imaginatively beautiful though physically impossible "flying gallop" so characteristic of later Plains Indian portrayals of the horse in motion. Cohoe could conceive of no other way of painting a running horse, so firmly fixed was this stylistic requirement. Like the horse, its rider is also true to traditional form as he sits with leg straight-kneed and slanting forward, body rigidly upright, his featureless face in simple profile, torso impossibly twisted a full ninety degrees to the left to show his full breast and two shoulders. Yet upon the framework of strict convention Cohoe has built individual detail appropriate to the man and the situation. The rider has shot his full quiver and is now arrowless. He has shifted his useless compound bow to his right hand, with

29

which he also grasps his horse's reins, leaving his left hand free to lash the flank of his steed with his saw-toothed quirt such as is usually carried by War Dance leaders.

This rider wears a silver ornament just above the waist, attached to the familiar Plains breastpiece of shell hair-pipes (turned out for the Western trade in a New Jersey factory). His headdress is a cluster of dyed animal-hair with two erect and two suspended eagle feathers. His two braids are wrapped differently, one with red and black cloth, the other with red alone. Over the sleeves of his long close-fitting green cotton shirt are wide German-silver armbands. Prominent is the long red breechcloth, a strip torn from across the width of a piece of strouding, or trade-cloth, with its white selvages. So characteristic was this garment that the pictograph sometimes used in denoting "Cheyenne" shows a man whose distinguishing feature is a full-length breechcloth before and behind, each end terminating in a white band. A black vest and leggings complete the rider's costume. The stripe and cut of the latter betray their origin as part of a U.S. Army uniform.

The other rider shows the Cheyenne "forked" style legging of buckskin fringed and embroidered with porcupine quills or trade-beads. He, too, has emptied his quiver and is dealing a death blow with pipe-tomahawk to a faltering victim which is drawn with a beautiful naturalism that breaks the stylized flow of elks and horses across the page.

In 1874, when Cohoe was hunting on the Southern Plains, white-tailed deer, pronghorns, and buffalo were still abundant;

turkeys occurred in almost unbelievable numbers. The open forest region of the Rocky Mountains of Colorado, the territory of Cohoe's birth and early boyhood, and even the Wichita Mountains of Oklahoma (as late as 1852) were the habitat of the elk depicted here by Cohoe, himself the animal's namesake. This majestic beast is readily recognized by his light rump-patch, stubby tail, and spreading antlers.

The crude representation of rolling, tree- and grass-covered hills behind the flat plain surely fixes the location of a real hunt for the young artist, even though, with no traditional precedent for such forms in aboriginal Indian painting, he has failed artistically in the effort.

PLATE THREE: BUFFALO

III. *Buffalo*

CURIOUS AS IT MAY SEEM, in view of the importance of the buffalo (called "bison" by the purists) to all the Plains tribes, this animal is rarely found in old-time hide paintings. Even as in the drawing of turkeys, Cohoe was wholly on his own in painting his impressive scene of the running slaughter of a stampeding herd. In a previous hunting scene he had solved his personal problem of picturing the pronghorn and the running dog by making them basically similar to horses. But here, when he tried to turn a long-legged horse into a running buffalo, a monstrosity resulted. And yet he did not really fail. A stampeding herd moved with the heavy, thundering bulk of a dark cloud upon the land. Where pronghorns, horses, and elk leap in light-footed flight across the other scenes, this drawing gives us the feel of a wild massiveness in which even the horses have lost their usual free-soaring quality.

In true Cheyenne fashion the riders have forced their way into the very heart of the herd for their close-in shots. This was

35

the way it was done when they had only bows and arrows or spears with which to bring down their quarry. A man shot across the left side of his horse's neck, seeking to send his shaft home between the ribs. Even those hunters armed with guns are carrying on the old pattern. Buffalo horses were trained to run close to the right haunch of the selected game, exactly as Cohoe has pictured them here. Nor did they have to be guided by the reins.

On the flanks of the herd, a boy depicted upon a small yellow pony has sent one fatal arrow through the vitals of a yellow buffalo calf which he has cut out for his own kill. The death arrow is about to follow.

"When I was ten years old in Indian Territory," wrote Cohoe's fellow captive Roman Nose, "I commenced to kill buffalo calves, shooting them with bow and arrows, and then when I grew up about fourteen years old, I had killed big buffalo good many."[1]

This could be Roman Nose's first buffalo calf.

[1] Henry C. Roman Nose, "An Indian Boy's Camp Life," *School News* (Carlisle Barracks, Pa.), Vol. I, No. 1 (June, 1880), 1.

PLATE FOUR: FLAYING THE BUFFALO

IV. *Flaying the Buffalo*

WITH THIS SKETCH Cohoe abandons the customary portrayal of action. The excitement of the chase is over. The hunter has tethered his horse, laid his quiver upon the ground, removed the arrows (one broken) from the stricken carcass, and partly stripped off the hide.

This fixed scene gives opportunity to concentrate on details. The quiver on the ground shows a large cylinder for the arrows, which is attached to a longer but narrower bag to hold the bow separately. A carrying strap passes between the two segments at two places for better balance. A pointed, decorated flap—with no purpose other than ornamentation—hangs from the mouth of the quiver. Fringed at top and bottom, such a case would have been an ornamental appendage to any man.

The hand of the observer on the left that seems to hold the saber bedecked with otter-skin streamers and pendent feathers must have first been intended to hold the umbrella. Cohoe could have added the saber as an afterthought as a name-symbol for the observer in the manner of the old-time pictographs.

The successful hunter has girded his robe for the job at hand; the upper part of it has been turned down below his waist-line. A German-silver ornament with three dangling silver crescents hangs down from his hair-pipe breastplate. The butchering is under way: he has severed the hide down the backbone, turning the loose skin down to the belly. Blood from the beast's punctured lungs still oozes from its mouth and nostrils.

These is something special about this flaying. Just what, cannot be said. But that it concerns the killing and preparation of no ordinary buffalo is evident. The animal itself is drawn with a skill that transcends Cohoe's achievement with the common herd in the hunt scene. Intent interest is achieved by focusing all faces, of men and horses together, upon the rigid central figure, which, for its part, glares straight up at the viewer. A notable circular composition, unusual in any Indian painting, adds to the impressiveness of the effect. The imposing mounted personages at the two sides reveal the dignity of the occasion. The hunter's horse, because it is partially obscured and smaller than that in the foreground, gives perspective depth. The circle is closed, lightly but firmly, by the bow and arrows upon the ground. We look at an angle from on high into a pit of death for the buffalo.

PLATE FIVE: THE SUN DANCE

v. *The Sun Dance*

THE SUN DANCE was one of the three great tribal ceremonies of the Cheyennes, the other two being the Medicine Arrow Renewal and the Crazy, or Animal, Dance. It was a ceremony of world renewal through which the exhausted energy of the universe was recharged by imitative ritual acts. It was, therefore, extremely sacred and impressive, its origin rooted in mythological times of long ago.

There are two major parts to the Cheyenne Sun Dance, which is still performed annually by both the Northern and the Southern Cheyennes. Four days of secret world-renewal rituals are performed by the priests in a lodge called the "Lone Tipi." These are followed by four days of public dancing in the Sun Dance lodge proper. This is what we see in Cohoe's picture.

The true lodge is formed of a series of upright, forked posts forming a circle about a much larger forked center pole. Stringers run from the crotch of the center pole to each of the peripheral uprights. A bundle of dogwood and cottonwood brush reposes

43

in the center-pole crotch. Cohoe depicts only the outer delineations of the lodge and simplifies the problem of draftsmanship by use of a hanging lining that would obscure the other poles. His composition takes an ordered rigidity in keeping with the ceremonial character of the occasion. Dancers and spectators are grouped by types in perfectly horizontal or vertical lines.

Dancers are adorned for the day's ceremonies, each pair painted by a different instructor. The first two, carrying medicine wheels, wear yellow paint with blackened lower legs and forearms, and a design in black to represent the sun with rays. The second pair have crescents on their yellow backs and leather shoulder-belts tied at the waist. One wears his hair unbraided. The others have purple bodies with red on lower legs, forearms, and waists, and white crescents. Strips of willow bark with leaves attached serve for wreaths, shoulder-belts, wristlets, belts, and anklets. Connected to the hand of one of the dancers by the conventional line denoting ownership is the horned and tailed bonnet identifying him as a warrior of distinction. Lance, shields, and headdresses indicate the rank of other devotees. Interesting is the view of a small head roach (above the right-hand shield) from the under side, showing its construction.

Drummers and singers are grouped about a stiff rawhide sheet drum in their traditional place to the south of the entrance to the lodge. The unusual and effective portrayal of the features of the middle of the three singers facing outward reveals that Cohoe's failure ordinarily to show facial details is, indeed, adherence to the stylistic conventions of primitive Plains painting rather than a lack of technical skill. But why should this one person receive such favored attention? Could it be a self-portrait commemorating some far-off Sun Dance at which Cohoe, the young warrior, had a front-row seat?

An important feature of every Sun Dance was the ceremonial piercing of the ears of three- to six-month-old babies. A revered warrior was called into the lodge between dances. There he counted coup, after which the infant's ears could be slit for decorative rings. The babe in the beaded bag on the cradleboard is very likely awaiting such an event, while the warrior with tomahawk, standing in the lower left, will use the weapon to count his coup even as he had struck the enemy with it in battle.

The multiplicity of umbrellas—complete with floating eagle feathers—suggests a brisk business for traders in the late 1800's. Umbrella handles appear to be tucked between the blanket and shoulder blade, freeing the arms to clutch robe or fan. The man near the upper left corner has furled his umbrella so that only the curved handle-end protrudes. The outsize sunshade at the right shelters a pair who may well be foreign dignitaries. Top-knot of stripped feathers, elaborate "crown" hat, novel design on the legging, and face paint set them apart from the other spectators.

The three women seated at the left of the dance lodge, including the baby's mother, may be recognized by the absence of such masculine attire as feathers, breastplate, beaded blanket-strip, and a pair of wrapped braids. They wear hair-pipes both as

45

chokers and in vertical strings. The mother wears knee-length leggings beaded and painted in a way that may indicate her husband's war honors. A fourth woman stands in the right foreground with the tip of her conch belt below her wrapped robe. Women were welcome spectators at the Sun Dance, and the wives of the head priest and the pledger of the dance had important ceremonial parts to play in the ritual itself, even though no women were numbered amongst the dancers.

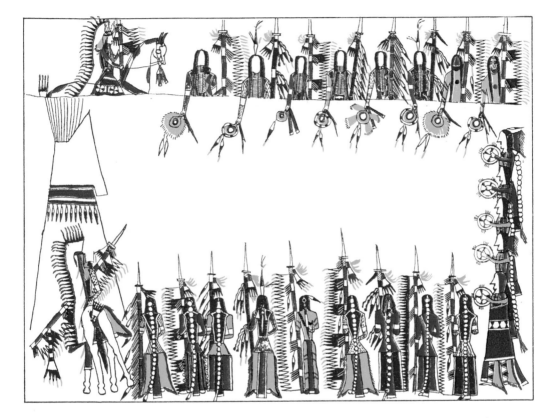

PLATE SIX: WOLF SOLDIERS

VI. *Wolf Soldiers*

THIS RESPLENDENT SCENE portrays a military society dance held in connection with the Sun Dance. During the four preliminary days of the secret Lone Tipi rites, the pledger of the Sun Dance was joined in the tipi by the members of his soldier band, who sang and danced with him to express their fraternal loyalty.

The gaily colored group dancing in opposing rows under the direction of their two mounted masters of the dance is a body of Wolf Soldiers. This society had been founded in about 1815 by Owl Man after a wolf vision had told him how to do so. In their dances the Wolf Soldiers carried full-feathered lances as well as doughnut-shaped hide rattles embellished with clipped horsehair and feathers. Their dignified dance was done in an erect position by jumping up and down with their heavy lances in slow rhythm.

In this dance, three of the participants are themselves Sun Dance pledgers, naked except for G string and bustle strip.

49

George Bird Grinnell tells us: "During the first dance only the soldiers stood; when the second song began, however, the Medicine Lodge makers rose and joined them."[1] Facial and body paints are very important in sun dancing; Cohoe has again broken through the old-time convention of not showing facial features to detail the physiognomy and facial painting of the two pledgers in the upper right-hand corner, in addition to the body paints of both these men and the pledger (who wears a string of mescal beans slung bandolier-like over his left shoulder) in the middle of the bottom row. Two of them show front and back views of the paint of the Wolf Soldier Society—a yellow background with red applied on the chin, up the sides of the cheeks, across the forehead, on hand and foot, and in diagonal stripes on arm and leg.

All three of the pledgers are wearing the Sun Dance insignia of sun and crescent moon as well as "Yellow Paint," also called "Fifth Day Paint." This is worn on the *first* day of dancing in the Sun Dance lodge, after the conclusion of the four days of rites in the Lone Tipi. Cohoe is showing the final dance of the Wolves in support of their three members who are already painted to enter the Sun Dance lodge to begin four days of public ritual. The other soldiers will change to Sun Dance paint when this dance is finished, and they will join the pledgers in the Sun Dance proper.

Five venerable members, too old to join war parties any longer, are providing rhythmic accompaniment to their songs

[1] *The Cheyenne Indians* (New Haven, Conn., 1923), II, 227.

as they beat upon the small single-headed drums of the Wolf warriors, held high in their left hands. The two mounted dance directors have been chosen for their task in honorific recognition of their outstanding bravery. Each is entitled by his valor to wear a horned war bonnet with eagle feather trail similar to that shown in the Sun Dance picture. From the bonnet hang strips of weasel fur with black-tipped tails. All is sedate and orderly.

In projecting this scene, Cohoe has hit upon an interesting device. He wished to present the idea of an open square, while at the same time picturing the dancers as viewed from only a slight elevation. To achieve this effect he has drawn the horizontal line cutting off the lower halves of the upper row of figures—just as this part of their bodies would be cut off from the view of a spectator standing behind the lower row. He has also invented his own way of showing a horse from the rear: tilt the rump so as to get in all four legs!

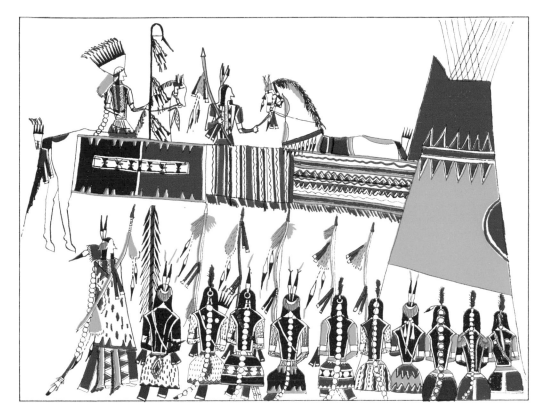

PLATE SEVEN: THE HONORING

VII. *The Honoring*

Dᴜʀɪɴɢ ᴛʜᴇ sɪxᴛʏ ʏᴇᴀʀs after Owl Man's wolf vision his society took on a new coloring. The wolf aspect faded, and in its place appeared another symbol, a strung bow-lance. The owner neither shot nor speared nor danced with it, but carried it as a badge of office in the new Bowstring Society.

In an open space in the camp circle, the military society of the pledger of a Sun Dance raised the tipi of one of their members. This served as their headquarters as they policed the camp during the ceremony. Here they feasted together and sang and danced.

It was a custom of the Bowstrings, during lulls in the Sun Dance, to sit in a row under their sunshade and their tipi with its sides raised to admit the breezes.[1] In Cohoe's colorful scene they have summoned the owner of a crooked lance to come before them to receive honors at their hands. His otter-skin-wrapped lance terminating in a crook, together with his up-standing war bonnet of eagle feathers, proclaim his valor in past

[1] George Bird Grinnell, *The Fighting Cheyennes* (New York, 1915), 81.

55

battles and will protect him in wars to come. In recognition of his sterling qualities the Bowstrings are bestowing upon him a horse.

The head chief of the Bowstrings stands in dignified grandeur before his seated followers, among whom are six of the society's seven subchiefs. They all carry the symbol of the organization, the lance-headed bow decorated with feathers, hair, or clusters of weasel-skin strips, save one man who holds a red staff wound with otter skin to which is attached a double row of feathers. The seventh subchief is presenting the beautiful feather-decked gift horse to the mounted man bearing the crooked lance.

Prominent in this picture are the trailing hair-plates hanging down the backs of the warriors. Copied from Spanish bridle and saddle decorations, the disks were at first hammered out of silver coins by the Plains Indians. The plates were later carried in graduated sizes by traders, to be bound by thongs to the uncut scalp lock. Their length attests to the reputation of the Cheyennes for long hair—and the terminal ornament adds to the length. A number of the men wear two erect feathers, while others display the roach, downy red-dyed feathers of the eagle, or crescents with fringe-like drops. One (the second from the right) even sports gold, fringed dress epaulets. Truly, George A. Dorsey was right in observing: "Each member dresses as he is able."[2]

2 *The Cheyenne: Ceremonial Organization,* Field Columbian Museum *Publication No. 99,* Anthropological Series, Vol. IX, No. 1 (1905), 26.

56

The watching warriors are enjoying the bestowal of the gift horse on the man whom they have honored. Those at the extreme right are seated in the Bowstrings' tipi with its raised sides. The row of blankets extending from the tipi is a conventionalized representation of a sunshade made of blankets spread over horizontal supports held up by forked poles. The first blanket is the familiar bicolored strouding with binding and beaded strip, the second a self-fringed Navaho, and the third an article of trade.

Like the previous scene, this one is more easily understood if the viewer imagines himself to be looking down upon it from an angle of forty-five degrees. From there the sunshade would, of course, cut off from view the lower part of the horse group on the other side of it.

PLATE EIGHT: THE FEAST

VIII. *The Feast*

THE CROOKED LANCE OWNER who had been honored by the Bowstring Society is now returning the gracious compliment with a leisurely feast for the eight chiefs of the Bowstrings. The host is seated in the doorway of the tipi, ready to ignite his ceremonial pipe with the tinder-stick which his wife is lighting in her cook-fire. So will the feast be solemnly opened. The crooked lance and war bonnet, differing but little from those in "The Honoring," identify the host and his military rank. Some of his guests sit by a second tipi trimmed with buffalo tails, and this means that the host is a big man with more than one wife and one tipi. To the side is a tripod bearing evidence of his "medicine" powers: a medicine case of painted rawhide, and a sacred shield stripped of its cover and naked to the beneficent rays of the sun except for an otter-skin binding. The full-covered elk-tooth dress of his wife, her beaded pouch, silver wristlets, and trailing conch belt also attest to his social position. He is a great man indeed.

61

Impressive master of the whole drama is the head chief of the Bowstrings, regal in bearing and stature as before, towering over his followers. Lesser men have changed their raiment; he wears the same leggings and breechcloth as before, the same roach and trailing scalp-lock decorations, and the self-same robe. Like the others, however, he has left his bow-lance at home (for they are not now ceremonious). He has brought along his brilliant parasol and a fan—for it does get hot on a midsummer day on the Plains, and this is a strictly social call.

Recalling that these sketches are autobiographical, the viewer is led to assume that Cohoe belonged to the Bowstrings, and to speculate on which of these men is he. A youth of twenty would scarcely be one of the stars in this little scene, but even the extras have attained to the rank of subchief and are caparisoned to match the taste of our artist.

The first has a turban of otter fur with a pointed drop bound in red ribbon, with both parts appliquéd with beaded medallions. His neighbor wears a tasseled sash of yarn as well as a leather belt wrapped at intervals, and terminated, with silver. He carries a spontoon type of pipe-tomahawk to which is attached a streamer decorated in bands. A braided leather chain across the crown of the third man drops to his shoulders, where each end terminates in a feather and a weasel tail. The fourth man bears a bestreamered saber and smokes a tubular bone pipe. The last one displays on his head the stuffed skin of a small rodent.

To the left stands the tipi of the Bowstring who was a

purple-painted sun dancer in an earlier picture and a dance director in the dance of the Wolf Soldiers. His horned tail-bonnet is atop a pole, against which leans his spear. At the intersection of the two hangs his shield in its elaborate painted and feather-tiered cover. The inclusion of his gear links "The Honoring" and "The Feast" to "The Sun Dance." His tipi and the one at lower right display the lean toward the rear that was built into Cheyenne tipis against the heavy winds, while the tent in the upper right shows the skewers that pin the cover from smoke hole to door. Paintings such as the sun, moon, and stars were the individual designs of the owner, and held a certain significance for him.

Noteworthy are several points of Cohoe's developing artistic technique. He unifies the composition with the frame of tipis; he heightens the festive mood with bizarre colors; and he has learned to draw figures from the side.

PLATE NINE: THE OSAGE DANCERS

IX.   *The Osage Dancers*

I‍N THE LAST YEARS of the free life on the Plains the now popular War Dance, variously known as the Omaha Dance and
Grass Dance, spread throughout the tribes. The fact that Cohoe
shows the dance as performed by a foreign tribe, the Osage,
rather than by Cheyennes, raises the possibility that even as
late as 1875 the Southern Cheyennes had not yet made it their
own. Obviously, however, they were very interested in it, and
eventually they incorporated a new order into their system of
men's societies, calling it the Omaha Dance.

Among the Osages, the dance, which accompanied ceremonies preparatory to going to war, was itself a war pantomime.
Data on the components of the early Osage War Dance are
scanty: it included a dance "house" of some kind, large ornamental whips carried by the dance supervisors, crow-feather
bustles, head-roaches, weapons, and face-paint in stripes. A
white captive among the Osages some 150 years ago described
what he saw as follows:

"The warriors, arrayed in their military habiliments, at a proper signal, assemble and commence the dance. It consists in imitating all the feats of real warfare, accompanied with the alternate shouts of victory, and yells of defeat. In short, they perform everything that is calculated to inspire confidence in themselves and to infuse terror into their enemies."[1]

Cohoe's observant eye has noted traits of the Osages that were common to other tribes, such as their kinsmen the Omahas, who in the dance displayed regalia indicating the war honors which they had won: feather bonnet, either upstanding or with a tail reaching to the waist or the heels; one or more eagle feathers; tomahawk; or war shirt with fringe, decorated strips, and V-shaped bib. Some of the Osages followed the custom of the neighboring Pawnees in fastening a whole buffalo horn to the side of the headdress for the War Dance. Like the Pawnees, too, when they had donned their regalia, they repaired to a circular dance-ground enclosed by a low fence, where to the accompaniment of the one large drum they danced the all-male dance. They resembled the Oglalas in placing the big drum outside the circle of dancers, with high-ranking men seated by the singers, and lay members opposite. In the manner of the Crows they danced with an exaggerated bending of the body and lifting of the knees.

Typically Osage in this picture are the necklace of bear claws and otter fur, eardrops, peace medal, otter hat, long neck-

---

[1] John D. Hunter, *Memoirs of a Captivity among the Indians of North America* (London, 1823), 324.

lace, short breechcloth, beaded collar and garters, and leggings tight below the knee and cut with points projecting above. "Red Shaved People," the Cheyennes called the Osages. Their name in sign language denoted the concept "shaved heads." Cohoe faithfully shows the vermilion tonsure and ears that were their "national colors." The head is shaved except for a ridge of hair from crown backward to neck. The outer edge is cut short, but the scalp lock is allowed to grow and is sometimes braided into a pigtail called the "horn." Its use in anchoring hair ornaments securely is indicated in the rear view of the head-roach worn by the middle blanket-wrapped musician.

The Mexican blanket sunshade may have been suspended horizontally overhead or vertically at the rear wall of the dance enclosure.

PLATE TEN: ANASTASIA ISLAND

x. *Anastasia Island*

Wᴴᴇɴ ᴛʜᴇ ʜᴇᴀᴛ ᴏꜰ ᴛʜᴇ ꜱᴜᴍᴍᴇʀ ᴡᴀꜱ ᴏɴ," Captain Pratt wrote, "Colonel Hamilton, the Commanding Officer, allowed us the use of army tents, and we encamped on the ocean side of Anastasia Island. . . . A camp guard was established, more particularly with reference to keeping out of camp wild 'razorback' hogs which intruded at night."[1]

"They used to camp on the island and cook their meals out," recalls a Cheyenne who remembers the prisoners. "They caught those flying fish—the ones with the feathers—and roasted them over the fire, turning them on both sides. They tasted *good*."[2]

The island, just across the bay from St. Augustine and "covered with a dense growth of palmetto, oak, bay, Spanish bayonet and other underbrush,"[3] was most notable for its two

[1] Autobiography, MS in Pratt Papers.
[2] Miss Crooked Nose Flying Bird, oral communication to Karen Daniels Petersen, May 23, 1959.
[3] "Scenes in Florida," St. Augustine *Florida Press* (March 31, 1877).

73

lighthouses—an ancient Spanish structure and the new and towering American unit (165 feet) built in 1874. Although the two lighthouses were, in fact, a half-mile apart, they loomed so large in the vision of Cohoe that he has brought them together in a single frame. Of the old Spanish light, Doris C. Wiles has recently recorded:

"[The] date of construction of the stone tower is unknown, although it is generally conceded to have been late 17th or early 18th century. Governor Montiano is said to have remodelled an unconsecrated stone chapel on Anastasia Island for use as a guard house and lookout. . . .

"The United States government found the building in a state of neglect in 1821 but two years later Congress appropriated $5,000 for repairs and reconstruction. An oil lamp was installed and lighted for the first time on April 3, 1824. . . .

"A revolving light was first installed in 1855. During the Civil War, the light was removed. In 1867, however, a new lens and lantern were installed and the light re-established. The site was continually threatened by the sea during heavy storms, and the old light was found to be inadequate, as it was only 73 feet above sea level and visible for a mere 14 miles.

"Much difficulty was experienced in securing a site for the badly needed new lighthouse because of the confusion that existed in the old Spanish Land Grants, but in 1871 a site was selected about half a mile from the old tower. At this time only 35 feet remained between the high water mark and the corner of the ancient tower. Coquina jetties constructed for its protection until the new light could be completed proved insufficient to withstand the action of the sea. However, the present lighthouse was sufficiently completed in 1874 so that the old structure was abandoned. During a violent storm in June, 1880, the remains of the old Spanish lighthouse toppled into the sea."[4]

The sea wall pictured by Cohoe was of no avail.

In the camp-out scene on the island, the off-duty uniform of a United States soldier in the artillery service—sky-blue pantaloons, dark blouse, and fatigue cap—was the prison garb of the Indians. Although their costumes are somber by contrast to those in their ceremonials on the Plains, they cannot conceal the cheerful, lively gregariousness of the Florida Boys as they eat their army rations, supplemented, perchance, by their catch. Despite their change of clothes, the Indians still use their old squatting position as they eat before their pup tents.

[4] "Sentinels of the Coast," *El Escribano*, No. 51 (April, 1964), 10–11.

PLATE ELEVEN: WATER BUFFALO

xi. *Water Buffalo*

THE WILD BUFFALO CHASE on the Plains was a thing of the past for the prisoners in St. Augustine. Yet in Florida coastal waters they found a denizen new to them but fully able to test their skills and to fill their need for excitement, exercise, food, and sinews; they called it the "water buffalo." Crooked Nose Flying Bird well remembers the story: "They would go fishing, six of them. They took a big rope and all pulled on it. They caught a great big fish and wanted it for the sinew that was along its backbone. They wanted the sinew to make arrows, to tie on the feathers."[1]

How meticulous a representation is Cohoe's painting may be sensed from Captain Pratt's own record of the activity, revealed in his unpublished autobiography:

"There were a number of sailing yachts owned by citizens of the town; several of them were engaged in the business of

---

[1] Oral communication to Karen Daniels Petersen, May 23, 1959.

79

taking parties out sailing and fishing. Among these was a very large one capable of accommodating our entire party. The owner, a Mr. Pacetti, often interested his patrons by taking them on successful fishing expeditions. One feature of his programme was catching sharks. Very early in the day of imprisonment I engaged him to take our whole party to the north beach after sharks. When we reached the fishing place, which was just inside and along the deepest place entering the harbor, a very substantial post was set deep in the sand and the shore end of his heavy shark line tied to it. A big hook with a chain between the line and the hook [not overlooked by Cohoe] was at the other end. Eight to ten pounds of fish or meat on the hook was the bait. This was placed in the stern of his row-boat and the shark line coiled on top, and as he rowed into deep water the line passed out until he reached the end and then dropped the hook overboard. It was a favored place of the sharks in passing to and fro from the harbor. Sometimes the shark was stronger in the tug of war, and would successfully pull against the Indians until all the line was played out and the only [*sic*] fastening at the shore stopped him. It was great sport until the shark surrendered. Sometimes when they were pulling their hardest the shark would suddenly turn and dash toward shore and the crowd all fell down, and before they could get up the shark was going the other way. When finally he was tired out he was dragged up on the sand, flopping and squirming. Mr. Pacetti had a sharp axe and he showed the Indians how to kill the shark by sinking the axe into

80

the head. The Indians called the sharks 'water buffalo.' On one
trip of this kind we captured five, one of which Mr. Pacetti esti-
mated would weigh twelve hundred pounds."[2]

Cohoe has faithfully recorded what must have been a truly
exciting adventure. Captain Pratt himself, in his officer's uniform,
is the central figure of the scene but he is peripheral to the action.
He is there for the fun, and the prisoner with the pointed finger
seems to be running the show. Cohoe wants his viewer to know
that they got to the fishing spot in a sloop, but he is too much
of a plainsman to be concerned with the incongruity of leaving
the boat under full sail while the party is ashore. The men in the
foreground are not wading but are partially obscured from our
view by an ocean wave. The convention regarding distance indi-
cates the presence of a shark lying farther up on the beach,
rather than a missile in mid-air!

[2] Pratt Papers.

PLATE TWELVE: WAR DANCE AT FORT MARION

XII.   *War Dance at Fort Marion*

THIS POIGNANT PICTURE presents a visual image of the meeting of two cultures. The throng of somber, straight-laced, complacent Victorian ladies and gentlemen with their bustles, fans, and top hats has hemmed in the remnant of a people once colorful, free, and vigorous. Northern visitors looked upon the antics of the tamed savages with genteel condescension. One, a lady of literary pretensions, wrote of the Indian dances at Fort Marion: "In their movements the poetry of music, or motion, has no votaries; but a slight approach toward it is made, as they all take the Grecian Bend,[1] and keep it, while going through their gyrations."[2] A New York visitor responded to the theatrics of the occasion by recording: "At dark fires were again lighted in the open court of San Marco,[3] and the sea-wall was black with visitors

---

[1] The posture affected by fashionable ladies of the time: body bent forward sharply from the hips.

[2] Silvia Sunshine [Abbie M. Brooks], *Petals Picked from Sunny Climes* (Nashville, 1885), 213.

[3] An early name for Fort Marion, given by the Spaniards who completed it in 1756.

85

eager to witness an Indian war dance. It is a wild but monotonous sight at its best; but in the spacious court of this old crumbling castle the effects of light and black shadows produced by the fires against a background of decaying Spanish architecture, the wild creatures dancing around these fires, and the black and smoky sky above presented a weird and beautiful picture."[4] A third account, probably enhanced in the interest of propriety, spoke of the Indians "closing the evening with a genuine war dance in native costume—or rather its absence,—during the performance of which they became so excited that it was judged best to cause all the ladies to withdraw."[5]

Local reporters, with an eye toward the tourist trade, were more ardent. "About twice during the week the Indians hold a grand pow-wow, execute war dances, and sing their war songs."[6] "On the arrival of the excursionists . . . Capt. Pratt called upon the Indians to give a dance, which they did in good old Indian fashion."[7] "The Indian war dance, at the Fort, on Thursday night, was a magnificent affair, the best of the season. The acting was superb; the representations of battle scenes and death scenes would have done credit to the stages of the leading theatres of

[4] E. R. T. [Townsend], "Aboriginal Junketing, The Cheyenne Prisoners at San Marco on the Mimic War-path," New York *Daily Graphic* (January 6, 1876).

[5] M. E. Winslow, "Taming the Savage," New York *Observer* [1876].

[6] "A Glimpse at the Indians," St. Augustine *Florida Press* (July 3, 1875).

[7] "Return of the Excursionists from St. Augustine," Savannah, Ga., *Morning News* (June 28, 1875).

the North. The chiefs of the parties were Zo-tum and Ah-ke-ah, Kiowa warriors."[8]

Cohoe here pictures the "benefit" dance of March 13, 1876, the last noteworthy one until the closing weeks of imprisonment. Advance handbills announced: "Reserved seats—50 cents, To the Ramparts—25 cents. The amounts raised by admissions to the Fort will form a fund for the benefit of the Indian Prisoners, to enable them to furnish their School-room, &c." To this worthy cause two distinguished spectators lent their support. Between the dancers and the musicians stand Captain Pratt and Bishop Whipple.

The dancers wear such costumes as their captivity affords: paint on body and face, feather headgear, and breechcloth. This is not the usual long Cheyenne garment but the abbreviated one borrowed from the Omahas and Osages along with the War Dance itself.[9] One of the musicians seated about the drum wears the long breechcloth, while all are wrapped in dark strouding blankets with center seams along the white selvage. So popular was the performance pictured by Cohoe that "as early as seven o'clock the rush to the old Fort commenced. Omnibuses and carriages could not supply the demand. For two hours the travel continued, and at nine o'clock, every obtainable seat had been

[8] "The Indian War-Dance," [*Florida Press*?] (n.d.).

[9] Captain Pratt referred to the dance as "an Omaha dance given by the prisoners on the solicitation and to please their friends in St. Augustine as well as to amuse themselves." Memos, in Pratt Papers.

secured, while hundreds were obliged to stand. The parapets above were also crowded, and to make a correct estimate as to the number of spectators, would be almost impossible, but it was believed that Two Thousand people were in the Fort at one time."[10]

Reports of several performances combine to provide a unique eyewitness account of the War Dance of the Plains Indians, wryly called by one eminent spectator "a show at which few whites are ever present except as prisoners."[11] The dance is wedded to the art of drama, in characteristic Cheyenne fashion.[12] The War Dance emerges as a pantomime that is well compared to ballet.

On the Fourth of July, 1875, the prisoners fused their War Dance with the ritual observance of American Independence, an early expression of what is now a common American Indian practice.[13] A week later the *Florida Press* gave its readers the following glowing account:

"Blazing in the centre of the court yard was a huge bonfire, and seated apart, in a group, were Lone Wolf, Double-Vision, Heap of Birds, Medicine Water, Bearshee [Bear Shield], Long Back, &c., &c., who formed the grand vocal and instrumental

[10] "The Grand Gala Day!!" St. Augustine *Florida Press* (March 18, 1876).

[11] "Champ," Home Correspondence—date line, St. Augustine, March 18, 1878—Boston *Weekly Transcript* (April 2, 1878). J. Wells Champney was a popular illustrator of the day.

[12] Cf. E. Adamson Hoebel, *The Cheyennes* (New York, 1960), 77–79, on the Scalp Dance.

[13] Today the Northern Cheyennes hold their Sun Dance over the Fourth of July.

band. [These are the chiefs and subchiefs, who by custom acted as singers and drummers.] The music consisted in singing a low weird chant, which was accompanied by the drums, and at times was quite spirited; the dancers jumping up and down and keeping exact time. . . .

"At 8 o'clock the ball was opened—the braves being *en grand tenue*, painted and bedecked in the orthodox manner of the Plains—and seemed to enjoy the sport very much. . . .

"The grand concluding part of the evening . . . as announced by Mahmantee [a Kiowa chief] would be

AN OSAGE WAR DANCE.

"Soon the music struck up, and then appeared one, two, three, and successively the whole of the dancers, equipped in every imaginable fashion . . . and then began one of the most amusing, grotesque, indescribable performances ever witnessed." It was called elsewhere in the paper "a spectacle which filled every one with admiration and wonder. Every motion, every song, and every utterance in the dance had its meaning. The carrying off of the dead and wounded was performed exquisitely. Indeed everyone was impressed with the spectacle as magnificent."

"The Black Crook[14] was completely thrown into the shade, and the acting was superb. The dancing was kept up, with unflagging spirit, until after eleven o'clock, when the tired spec-

14 The most spectacular melodrama of the ante-bellum period, a play with music which broke all performance records in New York, boasted a *corps de ballet* of one hundred persons, and shocked the audience with its brief costumes (tights).

tators and performers bade each other a hearty good night, with many happy returns of the day we celebrate [July 4, 1875]. . . .

"We, by a happy combination of circumstances, were enabled . . . while doing honor to the occasion, to confer *real* happiness upon the three score and ten noble red men, confined in Old Fort Marion."[15]

The warriors of former days had found happiness on a stage enclosed by prison walls.

[15] "Fourth of July Celebration in St. Augustine," St. Augustine *Florida Press* (July 10, 1875).

1. SKETCHES

(Colored originals unless indicated otherwise.)

Crowe, F. Hilton. "Indian Prisoner–Students at Fort Marion," *Regional Review*, Vol. V, No. 6 (December, 1940), 7.

> Unidentified artist—2 black and white reproductions.

Curtin, L. S. M., Santa Fe, N.M.

> 1. Howling Wolf—28 sketches
> 2. Zo-Tom—28 sketches

Hampton Institute, Hampton, Va. Huntington Library.

> 1. Tsadeltah, Tich-ke-mat-se, Howling Wolf(?), Zotom, Packer, White Bear, Left Hand, Koba, Ah-sit, and unidentified artists—84 sketches from two books.
> 2. James Bears Heart—1 sketch.

Lanier, Sidney. *Florida: Its Scenery, Climate, History* (Philadelphia, c. 1875), 53.

> Unidentified artist—1 black and white reproduction.

Massachusetts Historical Society, Boston. Francis Parkman Papers.

> 1. Making Medicine, Bear's Heart, Buffalo Meat, Etahdleuh, Cohoe, Koba, and Tsait-kope-ta—28 sketches.
> 2. Unidentified artist—1 sketch.

Missouri Historical Society, St. Louis. Pictorial History Department.

> Wo-Haw—48 sketches from two books. Excerpts appear in: Mrs. Dana O. Jensen, "Wo-Haw: Kiowa Warrior," *Bulletin of the Missouri Historical Society*, Vol. VII, No. 1 (October, 1950), following p. 76—7 black and white reproductions; and "St. Louis Art Discovery," *Post-Dispatch* (St. Louis, Mo.), Sunday Pictures Section, Vol. CII, No. 332 (August 13, 1950), 5—5 colored reproductions.

Museum of the American Indian, Heye Foundation, New York, N. Y.
1. Zotom—2 sketches.
2. Bears Heart—24 sketches. An excerpt appears in: Marius Barbeau, *Indian Days on the Western Prairies*, National Museum of Canada, *Bulletin No. 163*, Anthropological Series No. 46, (Ottawa, Ont., 1960), 115—black and white reproduction.

Petersen, Karen Daniels, St. Paul, Minn.
Cohoe—16 sketches.

Robinson, Roy H., Chicago, Ill.
1. Etahdleuh—32 sketches.
2. Ohet-toint—31 sketches.
3. Bear's Heart—25 sketches.
4. Bear's Heart and Ohet-toint—26 sketches.

Rodee, Howard D., Columbus, Ohio.
Bears Heart—1 sketch.

Smithsonian Institution, Bureau of American Ethnology, Washington, D. C.
1. Making Medicine (No. 39a)—23 sketches.
2. Making Medicine (No. 39b)—21 sketches.
3. Koba and perhaps others (No. 39c)—21 sketches.
4. Buffalo Meat (No. 4656)—16 sketches.

Smithsonian Institution, U.S. National Museum, Washington, D. C. Division of Ethnology.
1. Tich-ke-matse—22 sketches.
2. Etahdleuh Doanmoe—4 sketches.
3. Wo Haw (Nos. 30747 and 30750)—2 sketches. Black and white photographs (B.A.E. Negs. 363b—1 and 2, Bear's Heart and Wo Haw, respectively) of two formerly in this group are on file at the Bureau of American Ethnology.

Walsh, Anthony, Montreal, Quebec.
Koba—17 sketches.

Yale University, New Haven, Conn. Beinecke Rare Book and Manuscript Library, Western Americana Collection, General Richard H. Pratt Papers.

1. Charles Ohet-toint—55 sketches.
2. Etahdleuh—37 sketches; black and white negatives of 8 Etahdleuh sketches.
3. Zo-tom—22 sketches.
4. Bears Heart—11 colored transparencies of sketches, and black and white negatives of them.
5. Making Medicine, Bears Heart, Nick, E-tah-dle-uh, Ohet-toint, Zotom, Cohoe, Little Chief, Chief Killer, Koba, White Man, Howling Wolf, Toun keuh, Squint Eyes, Zone keuh, Buzzard, Roman Nose, Shave Head, White Goose(?), and Soaring Eagle—44 sketches.

2. MISCELLANEOUS ART

American Museum of Natural History, New York, N. Y. Cheyenne Collection.

Ahsit (Whiteman) (No. 1.4616)—Fan with hunting scenes.

Hampton Institute, Hampton, Va. College Museum.

1. Koba (No. 1923)—Plaque with buffalo and men.
2. Koba (No. 1925)—Fan with camp and war scenes.
3. Etahdleuh (No. 1926)—Vase with warriors.

St. Augustine Historical Society, St. Augustine, Fla. Library.

Making Medicine and/or Little Medicine—Fan with Indians.

Smithsonian Institution, Bureau of American Ethnology, Washington, D. C.

Koba (No. 39c)—List of picture-words.

Yale University, New Haven, Conn. Beinecke Rare Book and Manuscript Library, Western Americana Collection, General Richard H. Pratt Papers.

Buffalo Meat—Colored transparency of illustrated list, entitled "Price Current."

Adobe Walls, Battle of: 4
Ah-ke-ah: 87
Ahsit: 91, 93
Anastasia Island, Florida: 21, 73ff.
Antelope: 26
Arapaho Indians: 6, 18

Barbeau, Marius: 92
Bauman, Mrs. D. R.: 10
Bear Shield: 88
Bear's Heart: 4, 91ff.
Big Moccasin: 5
Bison: *see* buffalo
Black Bird: 16
Black, Jay: 19
Broken Leg: 6; *see also* Cohoe
Brooks, Abbie M. (Sylvia Sunshine):
    85n.
Buffalo: 39ff.
Buffalo Meat (personal name): 91ff.
Butchering: 38f.
Buzzard (personal name): 93

Carlisle Indian School: 14
Champney, J. W.: 88n.
Cheyenne Indians: 3ff., 15f., 30, 35,
    43, 56, 87f.

Chief: 56, 89
Chief Killer: 93
Cohoe (William): 6, 12ff., 25, 29ff.,
    62f., 67, 79ff., 91ff.
Cohoe, Bruce: 16, 19
Cohoe, Mrs. Bruce: 16f.
Cohoe, Charles: 16
Comanche Indians: 4, 6
Costumes: 30, 44ff., 49ff., 56, 61f.,
    68f., 75, 87
Coup Counting: 25, 45
Cripple: 6; *see also* Cohoe
Crooked Nose Flying Bird, Miss: 73n.,
    79
Crow Indians: 68
Crowe, F. Hilton: 91
Curtin, L. S. M.: 91

Dances:
    Animal Dance (Cheyenne), 43
    Omaha (Grass) Dance, 67f., 87
    Osage Dance, 21, 67ff., 89
    Sun Dance, 20, 49ff., 55, 63
    War Dance, 18, 20, 30, 43ff., 67, 87f.
    Wolf Society Dance, 49ff.
Daniels, Asa W.: 12
Daniels, Hortense: 11, 13

Daniels, J. W.: 10ff.
Darlington Agency: 5
Deer: 30
Dog, portrayal of: 35
Dorsey, George A.: 56
Double-Vision (personal name): 88
Drum: 44, 51, 68, 89

Ear Piercing: 45
Elk: 29ff.
Etahdleuh: 91ff.

Feasting, ceremonial: 61ff.
Fishing: 79ff.
Fort Marion: 6f., 13; dances at, 85ff.
Fort Sill: 6
Fort Supply: 16
Fraternities:
    Bow String Society, 55ff.
    War Dancers Society, 18
    Wolf Society, 49ff.

German (Germaine) Family, killing of: 5
Gift giving: 55ff.
Grey Beard: 5
Grinnell, George B.: 50, 55n.

Hampton Institute: 13, 15, 91, 93
Headdress: 30, 44f., 51, 56, 61ff., 67ff., 87
Heap of Birds: 88
Hill, Henry B.: 11, 13
Hill, Jared D.: 10
Horse: gift horse, 56; portrayal of, 29
Howling Wolf: 91, 93
Hunter, John D.: 68n.
Hunting: 25ff.

Independence Day, celebration of: 88ff.

Jensen, Mrs. Dana O.: 91

Kiowa Indians: 4, 6
Koba: 91ff.

Lanier, Sidney: 91
Left Hand: 91
Lighthouse, Anastasia Island: 74f.
Limpy: 6; *see also* Cohoe
Lincoln, Abraham: 8
Little Chief: 17, 93
Little Medicine: 93
Lone Wolf: 88
Long Back: 88

Mahmantee: 89
Making Medicine (personal name): 91ff.
Medicine Water: 4, 88
Medicine Wheel: 44
Messiah, Comanche: 3
Miles, J. D.: 5n., 6n., 14f.
Minnesota Sioux Outbreak: 5, 8
Missions, Indian: 8f.
Mohe: 4ff.; *see also* Cohoe

Native American Church: 18
Nohnicas: 6; *see also* Cohoe

Ohet-Toint: 92f.
Omaha Indians: 87
Osage Indians: 67ff., 87
Owl Man: 49, 55

Packer: 91
Painting, hide: 25, 35
Pawnee Indians: 68
Pelican Woman: 16
Peyote Cult: 18
Pipe: 62
Plain Looking: 4
Pratt, Mason: 15
Pratt, Richard H.: 7, 9ff., 14, 73, 79ff., 86f.

Rambull, Mary: 19
Rattle: 49
Religion:
  Medicine Arrow Renewal (Chey-
    enne), 43
  Medicine Case, 61
  Medicine Wheel, 44
Robinson, Roy H.: 10, 92
Rodee, Howard D.: 92
Roman Nose (Henry C.): 36, 93

St. Augustine, Florida: 3, 8f.
San Marcos: see Fort Marion
Sand Creek Massacre: 4
Shave Head: 93
Shield: 44, 63
Short, surveying party, killing of: 5
Sioux Indians: 12; Oglala, 68; see also
    Minnesota Sioux Outbreak
Sketchbooks: 7, 9, 17, 19ff., 25, 91ff.
Sleeping Bear: 4
Small Woman: 16, 19
Soaring Eagle: 14, 93
Squint Eyes: 93
Standing, A. J.: 14
Stands in Timber: 16
Stone Calf, Mrs. Richanda Little
    Chief: 17n.

Tanner, George C.: 12
Tich-ke-mat-se: 91 f.
Tipi: 49, 55, 61, 63ff.

Toun Keuh: 93
Townsend, E. R.: 86n.
Tsadeltah: 91
Tsait-kope-ta: 91
Turkey: 25f., 31

Umbrella: 39, 45, 62

Vister: 16

Walking Coyote: 16
Walsh, Anthony: 93
Weapons: 44
  Bow, 29, 36, 40
  Bow-lance, 55, 62
  Crooked Lance, 55, 61
  Lance, 44, 49
  Medicine Lance, 25
  Quiver, 29f., 39
  Saber, 39f.
  Spear, 36, 63
  Tomahawk, 45, 62, 68
Whipple, Henry B.: 7ff., 17, 87
White Bear: 91
White Goose: 93
White Man (personal name): 93
Wichita Mountains: 31
Wiles, Doris C.: 74
Winslow, M. E.: 86n.
Wo-Haw: 91f.

Zone keuh: 93
Zotom: 87, 91ff.